ANIMAL STORY

GORILLA
MOUNTAIN

by Dougal Dixon

With thanks to our consultant,
Dr. Annette Lanjouw, Director of the International Gorilla Conservation Program

WATERBIRD BOOKS

Columbus, Ohio

ANIMAL STORY

GORILLA
MOUNTAIN

Children's Publishing

This edition published in the United States of America in 2004 by
Waterbird Books
an imprint of McGraw-Hill Children's Publishing,
a Division of The McGraw-Hill Companies
8787 Orion Place
Columbus, Ohio 43240-4027

www.MHkids.com

Library of Congress Cataloging-in-Publication Data is on file with the publisher.

First published in Great Britain in 2004 by *ticktock* Media Ltd.,
Unit 2 Orchard Business Center, North Farm Road, Tunbridge Wells, Kent TN3 3XF.
Text and illustrations © 2004 *ticktock* Entertainment Ltd.
We would like to thank: Richard Burgess, Jean Coppendale and Elizabeth Wiggans.
Every effort has been made to trace the copyright holders, and we apologize in advance for any unintentional omissions.
We would be pleased to insert the appropriate acknowledgements in any subsequent edition of this publication.

Printed in China

1-57768-897-X

1 2 3 4 5 6 7 8 9 10 TTM 09 08 07 06 05 04

The McGraw·Hill Companies

CONTENTS

KAGU, THE MOUNTAIN GORILLA

The air is warm and steamy. Suddenly, there is a rustling and crashing from the thick undergrowth. A small, black face appears. It is Kagu, a mountain gorilla.

Kagu is just a year old. He is the youngest in a family of ten gorillas.

When he was born, Kagu weighed just over four pounds, or about as much as a large chicken. For the first few months of his life, Kagu's mother held him to her furry chest. As he grew bigger, she carried him on her back. Now that he is older, Kagu plays in the undergrowth and climbs in the trees. His mother is free to search, or *forage*, for food. Kagu is never alone, though. The rest of the group is always close by. Mountain gorilla families do everything together.

Kagu is learning how to find food for himself. He will continue to feed on his mother's milk for another two years, though.

Kagu and his family live in the misty mountain rain forests of Africa.

There are fewer than 700 mountain gorillas left in the world, and they live in only two places.

About half of the mountain gorilla population lives in an area of protected parkland in the Virunga volcano range. This volcano range borders Rwanda, the Democratic Republic of Congo, and Uganda. The other half of the population lives in Mgahinga Gorilla National Park in Uganda, and Volcanoes National Park in Rwanda.

Kagu and his family live high in the Virunga volcanoes, about 1.7 miles above sea level. They live in the wooded slope of an inactive, or *dormant*, volcano.

In some places, the forest is thick and dark. Higher up the slopes, the land is more open.

Hagenia trees, large thickets of plants, called *stinging nettles*, and bamboo grow on the mountain slopes. Hundreds of species of birds live in the forest. Small antelope, called *duikers*, scurry through the undergrowth.

LIFE ON GORILLA MOUNTAIN

Kagu's father, Makono, is the leader of the group. Wherever Makono goes, the others follow.

If Makono walks, the family walks. If Makono sits down, the family sits down.

Like all adult male gorillas, Makono is known as a "silverback." The name describes the saddle of silvery fur that grows across his broad back and over his hips. Makono is 25 years old and weighs nearly 400 pounds, or as much as two or three people. Makono is the father of all four young gorillas in the group. It is his responsibility to protect the family and lead them through the forest as they forage for food.

In the midday heat, the family settles down for a nap. As they doze, Makono makes a gentle coughing noise. Scientists believe he makes this noise to reassure the group that everything is under control.

Kagu and his family spend their days looking for food. They wander around their home range, which is the wide area in which they live.

Plenty of vegetation grows on the forested slopes of the volcano, but the plants are not very nutritious. The gorillas must eat a lot of food to fuel their huge bodies. A big silverback like Makono can eat up to 66 pounds of vegetation in a day.

Mountain gorillas most commonly eat stinging nettles. They also eat bamboo, prickly plants, called *thistles*, plant shoots and leaves, and wild celery. Very little fruit grows here, but Kagu and his family will occasionally find and eat blackberries. In addition, mountain gorillas sometimes eat ants, worms, and young insects.

Gorillas eat with their hands and sometimes with their feet. They have powerful jaws and large grinding teeth. Their teeth help them to break up tough plant stems.

DIFFICULT TIMES

When mountain gorillas were first discovered a hundred years ago, people believed they were ferocious beasts.

Hunters came to Africa from all over the world to kill gorillas.

By the 1960s, conservationists and scientists realized that the mountain gorilla population was getting smaller.

The mountains where Kagu's family now lives were part of a national park. People from the villages were employed as park rangers to guard the forest and the gorillas.

Many local people did not want the authorities and the conservationists telling them what they could and could not do in the area.

Although hunting mountain gorillas was illegal, many people ignored the rules and continued to hunt the gorillas in the park. These people, called *poachers*, could make money by selling the animals, dead or alive, to people all over the world.

Kagu's grandfather lived in the forest during this time. His group was attacked by poachers. The park rangers tried to help Kagu's grandfather, but he died. They carried him back to their camp and buried him there.

For many years, people struggled to find ways to protect the gorillas while keeping everyone happy.

Over time, the conservation groups and the local people learned to work together. Gorilla poaching gradually stopped, and the mountain gorilla population slowly grew.

Then, there came a new danger. During the 1990s, a violent war broke out in the part of Africa where Kagu and his family live.

People fled into the mountains to escape the fighting. Soldiers used the thick forests where the gorillas live as a place to hide and attack rival troops. The people brought diseases into the forest, such as measles and the flu. Some of the mountain gorillas caught the diseases and died. Although the war is now over, the future of the gorillas is still uncertain.

Kagu and his family live in one of the most heavily populated parts of Africa. The park is surrounded by farmland. As the local population increases, people need wood for fuel and more land to grow crops.

NEW HOPES, NEW DANGERS

Kagu and his family are eating their leafy lunch when they hear voices in the distance. Makono quickly leads the group in the opposite direction, and the family disappears into the thick undergrowth.

The voices belong to gorilla tourists. They are on their way up the mountain to visit another group of gorillas.

These visitors come to the park and pay for the chance to see gorilla families in their natural surroundings. The money that is raised helps to support the local government and all of the villagers who work in the park.

Gorilla tourism is now one of the biggest industries in this part of Africa. It helps guarantee the survival of the mountain gorilla. If the gorillas are making money for their countries, then the local people and governments are more likely to protect them and their habitat.

It is getting dark. Now, it is time for Kagu's family to make a bed for the night.

The adult gorillas weave branches, twigs, and leaves together to make big nests. These will protect them from the cold ground as they sleep.

Tonight, Kagu and his family cannot sleep. Deep rumblings shake the ground all night. They can see a red glow in the distance. One of the active volcanoes in the next mountain range is spilling lava onto its slopes.

Then, the family hears human voices and shouting. People from the villages below are worried that the lava and hot ash may destroy their villages. They are climbing up Kagu's mountain to find a safe place to wait.

Kagu's family abandons its night nest and runs.

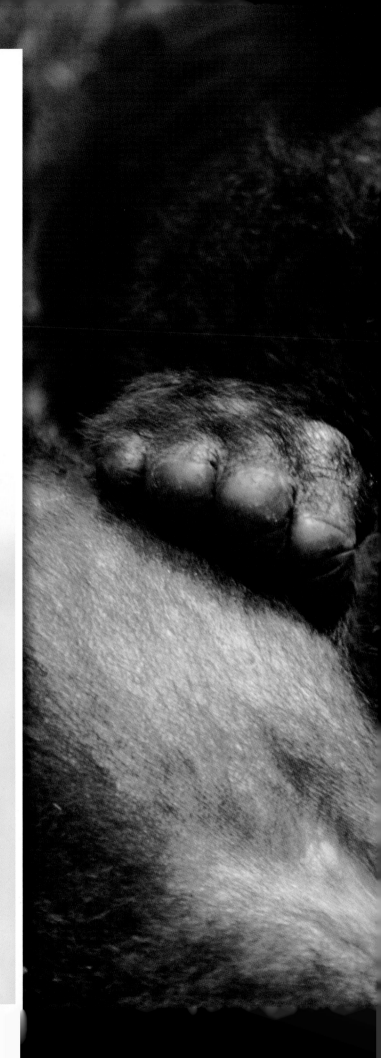

HIDDEN DANGERS

As morning approaches, the family moves higher up the mountain. Makono is in the lead. Kagu and his mother are at the back of the group.

As the family races through a dense clump of bamboo, Kagu's mother suddenly screams and falls to the ground. Kagu rushes to her side. He can see something wrapped tightly around her foot. His mother is caught in a poacher's trap.

The trap is a loop of wire attached to a bent bamboo pole. When Kagu's mother stepped on the wire, she set off a trigger. The bamboo pole sprang up, tightening the wire around her foot.

Poachers often set illegal traps like this one hoping to catch antelope or pigs. Often, other animals are sometimes caught in these traps. Every year, the park rangers find and destroy hundreds of traps in the forest.

Kagu's mother is in great pain. She pulls on the trap, but the wire tightens, cutting through her fur and into her leg. The family gathers around.

Suddenly, the family sees movement in the bamboo. Several people are creeping toward them. They could be the poachers returning to check on their trap. Makono does not hesitate. His group is in danger. He immediately positions himself between the people and his family.

First, he runs from side to side, while tearing at the vegetation. Then, he rears up on his hind legs. He charges forward at the people, tearing at the branches around him.

He stands tall and beats his chest with the cupped palms of his huge hands. Then, he lets out a great scream and raises his fists to frighten off the intruders.

The people slink back into the bushes and head off back down the mountain.

GORILLA RESCUE

All night, the family waits.
They cannot help Kagu's mother,
but they will not abandon her.

At first light, they hear voices again.

The people who found them yesterday were not poachers. They were park rangers, checking to see how the gorillas had been affected by the volcano. Now they have returned, bringing a veterinarian with them.

Makono rushes at the men again, but they are not afraid. As Makono approaches, the rangers stand their ground. They form a barrier so that the veterinarian can creep toward Kagu and his mother.

The veterinarian has anesthetic, antibiotics, and surgical equipment in her backpack in case she has to perform an emergency operation.

It is very unusual for veterinarians to treat wild animals in their natural habitat. But mountain gorillas are rare. If they are injured or become ill, the veterinarians from the conservation organizations will help them.

The veterinarian removes the trap and treats the wound. If the rangers had not found Kagu's mother, she probably would have died from an infection.

The air is warm and steamy. Suddenly, there is a rustling and crashing from the thick undergrowth. It is Kagu playing in the bushes.

Life is returning to normal, and Kagu's mother is recovering from her injury. While Kagu plays, his family members are cleaning each other's fur and removing insects. Grooming is an important gorilla activity. It helps to keep the bonds strong between the members of the family.

In the past forty years, the mountain gorillas have survived hunting, war, disease, and even natural disasters. As the human population expands in this region, people will be living closer to the gorillas. This will expose them to human diseases. The need to create farmland will also grow, threatening the gorilla's habitat.

If the local people can find other ways to earn money, then the precious areas of remaining rain forest will survive. The mountain gorillas and the other animals and plants that live in the forest will be safe.

Makono reaches out his arm and grabs his son. It is Kagu's turn to groom his father. For now, life is peaceful on gorilla mountain.

MOUNTAIN GORILLA FACT FILE

There are two species (types) of gorillas—the western gorilla (whose scientific name is *Gorilla gorilla*) and the eastern gorilla (whose scientific name is *Gorilla beringei graueri*). The eastern and western gorillas are then divided into subspecies of lowland and mountain gorillas. The mountain gorilla (*Gorilla beringei beringei*) was discovered in 1902 by a German army officer named Oscar von Beringe. The mountain gorilla is a subspecies of the eastern gorilla.

THE WORLD OF THE MOUNTAIN GORILLA

Mountain gorillas live only in two small areas of protected forest in Africa.

About half of the mountain gorilla population lives in Uganda's Bwindi Impenetrable National Park.

UNGANDA

DEMOCRATIC REPUBLIC OF CONGO

RWANDA

AFRICA

The other half of the mountain gorilla population lives in the Virunga volcano range. There are three areas of protected parkland here:

- Rwanda's **Volcanoes National Park**
- Uganda's **Mgahinga Gorilla National Park**
- The Democratic Republic of Congo's **Virunga National Park**

HABITAT

- The cloudy, misty rain forests where the mountain gorillas live are home to duiker antelope, forest buffalo, golden monkeys, and hyraxes (small plant-eating animals that look a bit like rabbits, but are closely related to elephants).

- There are two active volcanoes in the Virunga mountain range and six dormant (inactive) volcanoes. Some of the volcanoes are over 13,000 feet high.

- Many plants grow in the forests where the mountain gorillas live—hagenia trees, stinging nettles, thistles, vines, bamboos, and giant lobelia.

Lowland gorillas live in Angola, Cameroon, Central African Republic, Democratic Republic of Congo, Equatorial Guinea, Gabon, Nigeria and Republic of Congo.

PHYSICAL CHARACTERISTICS

MALE

Average height: 3.25 feet to the shoulder

Weight: 300 – 440 pounds

FEMALE

Average height: 2.5 feet to the shoulder

Weight: 150 – 200 pounds

- Gorillas are the largest of all the primates.
- Mountain gorillas have longer fur than eastern and western lowland gorillas.
- The fur on a male gorilla's back starts to turn silver when he is about 11 years old.
- A silverback can have an armspan of nearly 8.25 feet!
- When standing on his hind legs, a silverback gorilla can be over 6 feet tall.
- In the wild, gorillas live for about 30 to 40 years.
- Each gorilla has an individual noseprint. This is similar to human beings having individual fingerprints.

DIET

- Mountain gorillas are mainly vegetarian. They eat stinging nettles, bamboo, thistles, plant shoots and leaves, and wild celery. They will eat blackberries and other fruits, though very little fruit grows in their habitat.
- Occasionally, mountain gorillas will eat insects, worms, and ants.
- An adult gorilla can eat up to 66 pounds of vegetation in a day!
- Mountain gorillas get most of the water they need from the plants they eat.

REPRODUCTION AND YOUNG

- Female gorillas have their first baby at around 11 years old.
- Female gorillas have a baby every three to four years.
- Newborn gorillas weigh about 4 pounds, or as much as a large chicken.
- Mother gorillas hold their babies to their chests until the babies are big enough to hold on for themselves.
- Baby gorillas need their mother's milk until they are about 20 months old, but they may suckle until they are three years old.
- Gorilla babies ride on their mothers' backs.

BEHAVIOR AND SENSES

- Most gorillas are highly intelligent, gentle animals.
- Mountain gorillas live in groups of one or two silverbacks, adult females, younger males and females, and babies.
- The silverback is in charge of the family. He fathers most of the young and protects the family from other animals and human beings.
- When protecting their family or showing off to other males, silverbacks put on an agressive display. They charge from side to side, pulling up and throwing vegetation. They will also stand on their hind legs and beat their chests with the cupped palms of their hands.
- Most young male gorillas leave their birth group when they are about 11 years old. They live alone until they are able to start their own group. This usually occurs when they are about 15 years old.
- Young female gorillas leave their birth group and join a new group when they are about eight years old.
- If gorillas are threatened, they will make loud roaring and screaming noises.
- At night, mountain gorillas sleep in nests that they make on the ground from leaves and branches.

CONSERVATION

All gorillas are now critically endangered. There are just 10,000 western lowland gorillas, 7,000 eastern lowland gorillas, and fewer than 700 mountain gorillas left in the world.

SAVING THE MOUNTAIN GORILLA

- Mountain gorillas were once hunted almost to extinction. In the 1960s, primatologist (a scientist who studies primates) George Schaller and, later, Dian Fossey went to Africa to study the mountain gorillas. Although areas of the forest had been protected since 1925, it was only at this time that much effort was made to stop the hunting and poaching that was occuring. Many local people did not like the outsiders telling them what to do with their land. They did not all agree with the work of the primatologists and conservationists. But, the efforts of people like George Schaller and Dian Fossey brought the plight of the mountain gorillas to the world's attention and played a huge part in saving them.

HELPING THE MOUNTAIN GORILLAS

- The mountain gorillas live in one of the most heavily populated areas of Africa. As the human population increases, the need to cut down the forests to create farmland grows each year. The people who live on the edges of the parks have very little money, so conservation groups are working with them to find other ways to produce food and earn money.

- While mountain gorillas are now rarely hunted by poachers, they sometimes get tangled in illegal traps set for animals, such as pigs and antelope. Each year, the park rangers find and destroy hundreds of traps in the parks.

- Conservation groups are encouraging local people to farm and eat new types of meat, such as rabbits and goats, so that they will not set traps in the park.

- In 1986, the Mountain Gorilla Veterinary Project was established. It is very unusual for vets to treat wild animals in their natural habitat. Mountain gorillas are so rare, though, that if one is injured or becomes ill because of something that human beings have done, the vets will treat them.

- Protecting the mountain gorillas also helps to safeguard the habitat of other animals and plants that live in the mountain rain forest.

- Most of the gorillas found in zoos are western lowland gorillas. No mountain gorilla has ever survived in captivity.

GORILLA TOURISM

- Tourists come to Africa and pay to visit the mountain gorillas in their forest home.

- The idea behind gorilla tourism is to give governments a good reason to protect the gorillas. Gorilla tourism is now Uganda's third biggest industry, making $3.6 million a year.

- Trackers lead the visitors to the habituated groups (gorilla families that have gotten used to the presence of people). They follow gorilla clues, such as bent branches, nibbled leaves, and the smell of the silverback.

- Only eight visitors at a time are allowed to watch the gorillas, and they can stay only for an hour.

- Visitors must stay at least 23 feet from the gorillas.

- Mountain gorillas seem to be more fragile than lowland gorillas. They can catch human diseases.

GLOSSARY

ACTIVE VOLCANO A volcano that erupts from time to time.

ANESTHETIC A drug or gas used to make an animal or person sleep. It is normally used during operations.

ANTIBIOTICS Substances, such as penicillin, that are used to treat infections.

CONSERVATION GROUPS Organizations that care for the environment and campaign for the protection of wild animals. Their work can involve many different activities. They campaign against the hunting of endangered animals and study wild animals to find ways to help them in the future. They also work with governments to pass laws that protect the environment.

CONSERVATIONISTS People who work for conservation groups. Often, they are scientists.

DORMANT VOLCANO A volcano that is not currently erupting but has the potential to erupt in the future.

FORAGE To search for food.

HOME RANGE The area in which an animal will live over the course of many months or years.

NATURE RESERVE (PARK) Areas of natural habitat that are protected by laws so that wild animals can live there safely. In the parks,

hunting and setting traps are illegal, and the reserves are guarded by park rangers. Tourists can visit the parks to watch and photograph the animals.

NUTRITIOUS Having a large amount of vitamins, minerals, or other nutrients that an animal or human being needs in order to grow and be healthy.

PARK RANGERS Special guards that are employed by governments or conservation groups to work in nature reserves. These rangers, who work in the parks where the mountain gorillas live, keep records about the lives of the gorillas. They track births, deaths, and where different families are living. They also try to find and remove traps that have been set by poachers.

POACHERS People who illegally kill animals or take them from their natural habitat.

PRIMATES An animal group that includes monkeys, apes, prosimians (animals such as tarsiers and lorises), and human beings.

SILVERBACK The lead male in a family or group of gorillas. Usually he is the largest and strongest male and has won his position by fighting off rivals. Silverbacks father most of the babies in their group.

INDEX

PICTURE CREDITS

t=top, b=bottom, c=center, l=left, r=right, OFC=outside front cover, OBC=outside back cover

Alamy: 6lc, 10c, 11b, 20-21, 22t, 22b, 24-25b, 26-27. Digital Vision: OFC, 1c, 4-5, 6-7b, 8-9, 14, 18-19, 23, 28, 29, 30, 31, OBC. Corbis: 15t, 15b. Nature Picture Library: 12-13, 24-25t. Frank Lane Picture Agency: 16-17. Steve Bloom Images: 6-7 (background).

Every effort has been made to trace the copyright holders, and we apologize in advance for any unintentional omissions.

We would be pleased to insert the appropriate acknowledgements in any subsequent edition of this publication.

The publishers would like to thank: The International Gorilla Conservation Program (IGCP, a coalition of the African Wildlife Foundation), Fauna and Flora International, and WWF — International.